LETTERS FROM THE FRONT

Captain Palmer's eye witness account of
The Retreat from Mons 1914

CHARLIE LLEWELLEN PALMER

Charlie is the grandson of William "Pedlar" Palmer. He was also born in North Wiltshire and lived in Great Somerford, also went to school at Harrow and also enjoyed in his youth polo, horses and hunting. He lives with his wife and four children near Andoversford Gloucestershire, and has had a career in financial services, founding a financial adviser company of which he is currently chief executive. He has worked on a two published pieces, The Beaufort Hunt Diaries 2004 and a piece on India called "Hunting the Ooty" 2012.

LETTERS FROM THE FRONT

Captain Palmer's eye witness account of
The Retreat from Mons 1914

Charlie Llewellen Palmer

Copyright © Charlie Llewellen Palmer 2014

First Published in 2014 as *Letters From The Front
Captain Palmer's eye witness account of
The Retreat from Mons 1914*

Charlie Llewellen Palmer asserts the moral right to be
identified as the author of this work

Photographs and illustrations belong to the Palmer estate.
Copyright © Charlie Llewellen Palmer 2014

All rights reserved. No part of this publication may be reproduced, stored in a retrieval system, or transmitted in any form or by any means, electronic, mechanical, photocopying, recording, or otherwise, without the prior written permission of the publishers.

A catalogue record of this book is available from the British Lirary

ISBN 1499516428

Book & Cover designer: David Paramore

Printed and bound in Great Britain by CreateSpace, a DBA of On-Demand Publishing, LLC.

CONTENTS

About the author	1
Background	17
The Battle	20
Hitler's part in the battle	26
Significance of the First Battle of Ypres	28
The Charm of the Letters	33
27th August 1914 *First letter from France - with section cut out by censors*	37
5th September *"I never realised war was like this"*	39
4th September *General Chetwode's great work*	42
14th September	44
16th September *Eustace Crawley going well*	45
The fight for Wyschate and the Battle of Messines	47
23rd October *Goodbye to the horses*	47
23rd October *Card*	53

3rd November *Covered from head to foot in German blood*	55
5th November – *Five days and nights without sleep*	58
6th November *14 days holding the lines*	61
7th November *A bitter post battle letter*	64
8th November *From Dranouter, West Flanders.*	69
Summary of The battle of Wytschate - Undated - Perhaps 12th November	72
12th November *723 dead in our trenches*	76
12th November – *Towns deserted and desolate*	78
14th November – *The blackest day of Chetwode's life*	80
20th November – *32 yards from the Germans!*	83
22nd November – *The terrible cold*	86
24th November – *They are all dead*	88
26th November – *…get at these inhuman bestial devils and wipe them out…*	89

7th December *50% mental casualties among officers*   90

APPENDIX 1   99

APPENDIX 2   100

"No one can realise what this war is unless he has seen it."
Letter from the trenches on Messines Ridge 3rd November

ABOUT THE AUTHOR

ABOUT THE AUTHOR

William Llewellen Palmer *("Pedlar")* belonged to the generation that had it hardest of all the generations. They were born at the summit and finished their lives in a Britain bankrupt and rationed recovering from her second world war. At the start they were heirs to the Victorian British Empire. The Queen signed her letters Victoria RI

Victoria Regina et Imperatix

They expected to rule and assumed the responsibility that came with privilege and power. But for one born in 1883, like Pedlar, what marks them out was not the gilded good life, but rather the course of events. Their life was determined by events like no other life in no other time in Britain before or since. They were called to defend their country as young men. They saw their friends and relatives suffer or die in the trenches, and

William Llewellen Palmer ("Pedlar")

1

as retirement loomed they watched in horror as their own children went through much the same experience in the second world war. As the French war memorials so often say

"...à nos enfants qui sont morts..."

All the pale horses of the apocalypse stormed through their lives. They witnessed revolution, war, famine, plague and national bankruptcy. Some generations never see any of that. Their's saw them all.

Pedlar was the second son of a wealthy woollen manufacturer called George Llewellen Palmer. General George was in the process of making a fortune in Trowbridge. He was always smiling in a diffident kind of way. With new found wealth came the good life

"If I were as rich as Mr Darcy,"

wrote Jane Austen,

"I would keep a pack of hounds and drink a bottle of wine a day".

Well General George did exactly that. He leased some country from the Duke of Beaufort and installed a professional huntsman to hunt his new creation "The Avon Vale Hunt".

"That great old sportsman, for so long a Master of the Avon Vale,"

Wrote a newspaper in the 1930's after the general's death. George moved into Lackham House, now the agricultural college outside

ABOUT THE AUTHOR

Melksham. His business prospered and he designed "The Prince of Wales Check" tweed for the best dressed man of the day, the future Edward 7th. General George had married the daughter of Trowbridge town's other great woollen manufacturer, Jack Gouldsmith. Between the two of them they now ran the two key woollen mills in Bradford on Avon. Young bride Madeleine Gouldsmith settled down and produced four children, while George brought in new partners, establishing Brown and Palmer and, later on, Palmer and Mackay.

The eldest son, Allen, was born in 1881, and Pedlar followed two years later, and a girl and then another boy came later. Pedlar took much the same path as Allen. He followed his brother to Harrow school, which was emerging at the time as a rival to Eton in educating future prime ministers. George had been there too and so it must have felt familiar despite the fagging and gang culture that was so prevalent at the time at these boarding schools. As Thomas Hughes narrates, in Tom Brown Schooldays,

> *"...so bear in mind that majorities, especially respectable ones, are nine times out of ten in the wrong; and that if you see man or boy striving earnestly on the weak side, however wrong-headed or blundering he may be, you are not to go and join the cry against him..."*

The boys ate in their boarding houses, run by the teachers or "beaks" and drank a weak porter beer in the absence of clean running water to drink. His own housemaster was a Mr Colbeck, a French teacher and intellectual who wrote books of instruction on the French language. The Headmaster at the time was the friend and mentor of Lord Curzon, the famous James (later Bishop) Welldon

LETTERS FROM THE FRONT

I have always been used to the best of things,
I was nourished at Eton and crowned at King's,
I pushed to the front in religion and play,
I shoved all competitors out of the way ;
I ruled at Harrow, I went to Calcutta,
I buttered my bread and jammed my butter,
And returned as a bishop, enormous of port,
Who stood in a pulpit and said what he thought.

Pedlar received the classic Victorian education for future leaders of the empire. The first thing that often happened at Public School was the moniker-nickname. Another Palmer was at the school at the time, as well as his brother, and so William was quickly changed to "Pedlar". That one was not difficult. Pedlar Palmer from Canning Town had just won the world bantamweight boxing title aged just 18 and was *"A pocket sensation"* at the time. And so Pedlar it was.

Harrow at the time may have been an unforgiving place, but gave ample opportunities for development of leadership skills. Tom Brown was told on entering the upper sixth

"you may have more wide influence for good or evil on the society you live in than you ever can have again."

Pedlar took up fencing as well as the usual sports of Harrow Football and cricket. He carved his name in the wood panelling of the "old schools" fourth form room, a few inches from Anthony Trollope's own self-carved name, and it remains there today, one of the most prominent among the thousands carved illegally in

ABOUT THE AUTHOR

that room, including Churchill's and Byron's. He continued his career there in relatively undistinguished fashion – making a total of 13 entries in five years in the weekly school magazine, for house matches played in, runs scored and fencing matches won. The final entry was a thank you in a list of donors of chairs for the new Speech Room.

In those days the boys applied to join the military straight from school, like university places today. Pedlar applied to the Royal Military School at Sandhurst and secured 18th place in the examinations for Cavalry. That was another entry in the Harrovian magazine secured. His father at the time was a Colonel, a keen yeoman (meaning part time or territorial) soldier with the Wiltshire Yeomanry, spending weeks away on Salisbury Plain each summer on exercises. Pedlar was being true to his background. His brother Allen had just joined up before him, and so it was the easiest of choices to make.

The tough training at Military College prepared Pedlar for a lifetime of service to King and Country. Pedlar took time off to go hunting with his dad and the Avon Vale, at home near Trowbridge, and "passed out" from the college a couple of years later in 1903. During your time at Sandhurst it was required then to choose your regiment. He decided not to join the Wiltshire Yeomanry, which Allen had joined to follow his father, but the 10th Royal Hussars - a dashing and historic cavalry regiment known as the Shiny Tenth. This choice would allow him to be posted immediately to India. The 10th had just spent three years in South Africa during the Boer War. They had seen fighting in the Transvaal and were helping with administration as that war came to an end. The regiment was in India at the time and the promise to the young man would have been of army leisure and action, which usually meant service on the North West Frontier, known as *"The Grim"*.

For the next ten years Pedlar remained in India with brief periods of leave back to muddy England. He enjoyed himself to the full with polo and pigsticking and shooting game. He joined in military exercises, administered to the Indians and moved very slowly up the ranks, as was common in the army at the time. In those ten years he made it from Lieutenant to Captain. And he did not waste his leisure time.

It was in polo that he excelled and he played in the famous 10th Hussars team that won the inter-regimental repeatedly and also the Indian Open. He reached the pinnacle of the sport and was considered one of the best players of the game. There were over 360 clubs in India at the time and the game was watched by masses in a way that has never been matched since, except in recent years in Argentina. He became famous for his polo playing. The 10th Hussars remains even today a very famous team. Indeed one polo enthusiast recognised my own name in conversation on the side lines at Cirencester Park over 100 years later –

"do you have anything to do with the Llewellen Palmer who won the Inter Regimental with the 10th Hussars in India?"

They won that tournament for record seven consecutive years running from 1904 to 1911.

He proved himself as a young man in India. When the regiment was serving at Gulmarg, Kashmir he rescued a drowning man, nearly succumbing himself.

ABOUT THE AUTHOR

Pte Rand incautiously rode his horse into the water, a little in advance of the others, with the object of getting into clearer water, which, nearer the bank, had become muddy. Mr Brocklehurst, who was riding next him, warned him of the danger of going into unknown waters, and having watered his own horse, retired to where the troop was forming up. Almost immediately afterwards, the sloping bank game gave way, and Private Rand and his horse were precipitated into deep water. The horse lost his foothold and rolled over on his rider, who could not free himself from his stirrups.

The shouts of the man, and the sound of the struggles of the horse, attracted the attention of Lieut. W. Ll. Palmer, who was commanding the squadron, and he, without hesitation, rode to the spot, flung himself from his horse, and dived in to the assistance of his man, who had by this time sunk underneath the horse, and could not get up. He was seized by the drowning man, and both were in imminent peril of their lives.

Sergeant Major Kin, a non-swimmer, shouted to the squadron, who where some distance away, and out of sight. "Any man who can swim, hasten here to rescue drowning men."

In response, Mr Brocklehurst and others galloped to the spot, and the former in a flash, followed Mr Palmer's example, and dived into the water, to assist his squadron leader. Fortunately, however, simultaneously with his gallant action, the strength and skill of Mr Palmer had enabled him to accomplish his object in releasing Private Rand from the still struggling animal, and in propelling him onto the bank.

There can be no doubt that his bravery and promptitude were the means of saving the life of a Tenth Hussar and that knowledge if other well merited recognition of his act is not forthcoming will reward him for the act, which was the cause of a bath, in icy cold water, damage to his clothes and appointments and the loss of his watch in the water, and which, apart from its intrinsic worth was greatly valued by him.

He followed the regiment around India, and served not just in the Grim. This included Dehra, where Elephants were used to hunt cheetah, in Simla around the Vice-Regal Lodge, toured Udaipur, Delhi, Calcutta and finally at Rawal Pindi in 1911.

Pedlar had mixed well with some of the key figures that came through later during the 1914 war. He played polo with Douglas Haig and made other contacts that would allow him to carry out his key liaison role late in 1914. He was obviously at ease with the aristocracy. His father had made a lot of cash and Pedlar was both educated and entertaining. He was a catch for the aristocratic young lady sent out to India on the rebound as part of what became known as *"The fishing fleet"*.

He met Alexandra (Andy) Carrington, the eldest daughter of Lord Charles Carrington, 1st Marquis of Lincolnshire in Simla. Champagne Charlie, as he was known, was a "Grandee" in the age of grandeur. He was a close childhood friend of Bertie, The Prince of Wales, son of Queen Victoria, who by 1901 was Edward V11. This sort of relationship that does no harm in life at any time, but in an empire country ruled, according to Edwardian Historian David Cannadine, by just 200 families, patronage was vital and here was the key. Charlie Carrington, was powerful, domineering and ambitious. He had recently been appointed Governor of New South Wales, and on his return was selected from the House of Lords for a cabinet position as minister for agriculture in Campbell-Bannerman's last Liberal government. The Carrington money

ABOUT THE AUTHOR

had came from banking. One Robert Smith of Nottingham had lent William Pitt some cash to continue his Napoleonic war, in return for a peerage. With subsequent elevation to the aristocracy came massive estates in Lincolnshire and Buckinghamshire and the family seat at Wycombe Abbey, where Andy was born.

Carrington is remembered in posterity for his daily diaries which detail many of the leading lights of the day. They are a fascinating if mechanical record of events of the time. Detailed gossip of the day about the Prince or King, their advisers, circle and other leading lights of the day is recorded, although not a single entry relating to his fourth daughter's birth. Instead there were a number of inserted letters of commiserations from friends that it was not the son and heir at last. The son did arrive at last, at the sixth and final attempt, and the diary duly fills with congratulations from The Greats of the day. Lord "Bob" Wendover came into the world in 1898, only to be mortally wounded fighting the Germans in France in 1916 aged 18. A bullet in the shoulder, gangrene in a dirty hospital-railway-carriage and distraught parents looking on all the while. And more commiscration.

Andy's mother was a society butterfly, a beauty called Lily Harbord. She had come from Gwdyor Castle in Wales and was said to bring luck to whoever she watched the Derby with. When Bertie, Prince of Wales, had a horse running called Persimmon she took her place and the horse duly won. The Prince asked her to be his next mistress, and Charlie sensibly took a position as Governor of New South Wales, well out of the way of the week-long house parties that formed the core of Bertie's social circle, fanned scandal (Tranby Croft) and bankrupted the hosts (Sir Christopher Sykes).

This was a backward career move but may have saved the reputation of his marriage. Out in Australia they made a modest impact. The Carrington Falls is a famous tourist landmark in NSW and there are other traces of his time there. He famously sent a gang of workers to the gallows for gang rape. The gallows were too shallow and nearly broke and the nine suffocated since their necks did not break. One even managed to get a hand loose and spent several minutes writhing – all recorded in more cold handwriting in the diary. It was a scandal at the time. Was Charlie partly culpable? We shall never know. His extensive memoirs barely mention his second daughter Andy who spent five years of her childhood being educated by a Governess at Government House, Sydney. In comparison whole months worth of entries are devoted to the daily progress of Bob, his sixth child and only son.

Charlie Carrington's second daughter Andy was adventurous. She had enjoyed the free and easy Australian years and remained to the end keen to explore and learn. She was also a society beauty of the time. But she had been sent out to India to find a husband. For girls still unmarried by their mid-twenties India was considered the best alternative to the dreaded Governess role. But she was also determined enough and arrived in India not just to fall in love with the right sort. She almost immediately set out on an expedition with two other young ladies to Kashmir, climbing 14,000 feet on the pass by Mount Haramukh, in Kashmir. The explorer Francis Younghusband wrote from The Residency, Kashmir to congratulate her arrival

"You are built in the mould of an explorer"!

In 1910 Andy married Pedlar and they returned to England. Andy had her man, and it was a genuine love match, if not at first then certainly later when tested by forty years of war and absence and

ABOUT THE AUTHOR

death. This love shines through in these letters.

There is a brief interlude with service in Ireland and manoeuvres on Salisbury Plain before war takes over and consumes their lives. Pedlar secured a posting with The British Expeditionary force, attached to a new regiment, the 9th Lancers. It was an obvious posting for the well connected Captain. The Indian Army anyway was to form the backbone of the British Expeditionary Force BEF and he had impeccable contacts from polo in India and was able to act in liaison with the Generals of the time – Chetwode, Haig, French and Roberts.

These letters are the crucible of Pedlar's career. Aged 31 this was his moment on stage. He quickly grasped the truth that an entire generation were about to discover. Instead of proving himself by leading men to drive out die Hunnen – "the Hun" from France he found the horrors of war

"We said goodbye to the horses"

And so begins in six words the start of a new form of artillery warfare. Phrases such as these dominate the diaries and have the noble Scott-of-the-Antartic-feel-to-them.

"For God's sake look after our people"

Pedlar writes

"This is the day for me – curiously it will be a big day in history too..."

on 30th June 1916 from the Somme, just a few hours before that dawn on the blackest day of all Britain's history. It is clear that he had had the wit to see the importance of many events including in September 1914 of the Marne Battlefield just north of Paris. It was critical to the world situation and to the remaining four years of the war as nearly all historians today agree. Pedlar grasped this fact, not just from the daily memos from the Generals but as an educated leader. The Germans could have broken through in 1914, but they lost their nerve at the crucial time when they imagined they were defeated. Just a handful of men, Pedlar observes, held several miles of his front line at the key Messines ridge when the Germans stopped attacking.

This was the only conflict in history where there was almost no real time communication between the Generals and the fighters. Before, the leaders themselves had been close to the combat. After, radio ensured effective communication. In this war of artillery many of the communications were by hand written note

*"You would give your message to a man,
and he would never be seen again"*

said one survivor to me in 1980,

"It was just like that all the time."

Pedlar spent a lot of time delivering messages and reporting on the situation and liaising throughout the war. Somehow or other he survived, and after this first six months optimism about his likely survival grows.

After this Great War Pedlar bought a house jointly with his sister in law, at Godmersham Park, in Kent. Previously it had been

ABOUT THE AUTHOR

the home of Jane Austen's brother. The share was with Andy's older sister Ruby, who had married Bill, the Earl of Dartmouth, a former MP who had come home from the front with malignant malaria. Probably together they suffered from if not quite shell shock then perhaps a lighter form of what is today known as Post Traumatic Stress Disorder. Pedlar had had most of his insides removed as a result of war wounds on the Somme. The doctors said they must both live outdoor lives in order to recover their health. Pedlar lived on milk and hunted hounds with two large milk bottles attached to his saddle. They both had children and helped each other out, sharing staff and entertainment while the husbands came and went in the military.

The house was dilapidated but was set in a beautiful park. There were ten children and most of the farm workers had served with Pedlar's 10th Hussars. Pedlar looked after the stock and Will Dartmouth looked after the crops. In 1928 Pedlar's father died and he moved away to farming in Wiltshire. When living in the grand Rushmore Park by Salisbury he took on masterships and hunted hounds at The Portman and The Wilton hunts nearby. With Andy they brought up four boys in the go-go years of the 1920's and 30's. It must have been happy times for them all. During this blissful period – photos and records are all out of doors in shorts and braces, smiling and mostly with animals. Their four boys joined the army and took postings overseas in India and Australia. This happy time was of course ended by yet more war, but they were not to know this at the time.

When it came Pedlar was too old to fight again. He had ended his career as a Colonel and he had bought The Manor House at Great Somerford, near Chippenham, Wiltshire. He had been brought up in the district and his father had left him land nearby in Grittenham including historic Great Wood. He added more land and set about farming. Manor Farm, West Street, Downfield and Angrove Farm – one farm for each of the four boys. Edgar was one of the farm labourers who worked the horses for Pedlar and lived to tell many stories about the 12 "merry men" who worked the home farm in the 1940's and 50's. The star worker was Kendal who kept and showed the pigs, winning at Smithfield. Fred Brind looked after the sheep, famously producing three generations of lambs in a single year from his Wiltshire Longhorn. When Pedlar wore his cloak, they all said he was in a bad mood, that when he carried the cloak it signified a better mood and an easier day. Because of the weak stomach he took special flour from the mill at Little Somerford.

Pedlar took command of the Seagry Home Guard in 1939. He helped to install the pill boxes that still stand like bronze age water tanks in the area. They remain, half concealed by grass on their tops and brambles around, concrete slits facing out over long since dismantled bridges over the river Avon at Somerford. He oversaw activities with a monocle and served in Chippenham as a magistrate Justice of the Peace. Andy helped in the village with the collection of scrap to aid the war effort and they watched their sons go gaily off to war as Pedlar and his own generation had done so naively 25 years before.

All four of Pedlar's sons served in North Africa when the war started. They had a reputation for sticking together and helped each other out during scrapes in Cairo. The fun filled evening pranks normally started in the Long Bar at the Shepherds Hotel. But two of the brothers were killed within 12 months in 1941 and 1942. Julian at Fort Capuzzo in Libya, and Peter in an elite unit fighting against the French in Madagascar. Peter was recom-

ABOUT THE AUTHOR

mended for a VC but Churchill was at the time trying to persuade the Free-French under de Gaulle to fight for the allies. Many people were unaware that other French were fighting alongside the Germans for the Vichy Regime. The publicity would have been embarrassing and permission was refused.

Pedlar really cared about this. He wrote letters to ask why and journeyed to London to argue the case. In truth their Peter's death was expedient to a small french garrison at San Diego anxious not to be accused of being turncoats. It was a meaningless campaign to stop a deep water harbour falling into Japanese hands. The French put up a token resistance and surrendered at the earliest opportunity. 900 of the 1,200 garrison immediately declared themselves allied to the Free French. He had been proud to fight alongside the French in the Great War, taking photos of *"The gallant Poilu"* and so his eldest son's death in such a futile cause must have been a crushing final sadness for him and Andy. A monument by the Church at Great Somerford records their loss. They had seen their generation of countrymen, friends and cousins die in the first war

> *"Darling this is awful, all my friends are dead"*

he had written at the end of one of his longest letters to Andy. Both he and Andy lost brothers in the first war. To go through that war again and watch their own children cut down as well marks this generation out from all others. Pedlar and Andy did not live to see any grand children. They lived on another twelve years. His his beloved Andy pre-deceased him and stricken by grief he followed just nine months later.

The current owners of the Manor House claim to sense the

presence of Andy on the back stairs. They know it is Andy, they say, because there is sometimes a scent around the back stairs. The last traces of the two war generation. Decaying Edwardian grandeur lives on in balustrades on the Manor roof, facing west to receive the coach and horses. Double doors, Adams the Butler, white gloves, crafted butter curls for the dining room table. Finger bowls and cleaning silver. Buckets upstairs in the corridors to catch the rain during storms. Pedlar really was born to the best of times but lived through the hardest of times.

BACKGROUND

12th Lancers - A tired approach to night billets. September 1914

These are the letters from Captain W.Ll Palmer (later Colonel) to his wife Lady Alexandra ("Andy") Palmer. The author was known by all, including family, as "Pedlar".

At the time of writing Pedlar was 31 years old with two young children, referred to only briefly in the letters. Pedlar and Andy had a very happy and long marriage, and they both died within the same year in 1954/5.

Pedlar was serving in the British Expeditionary Force, attached to the 12th Lancers as a Captain. The 12th Lancers had a key role to prevent the breakthrough during the first months of the Great War and Pedlar had a central role in that regiment, and was later mentioned in despatches for his part. These letters record what no historical facts can bring out. Poetry to the maths, they lay bare the emotion of one man, who struggled to write with his head, but succumbed to the hurt in his heart, particularly towards the end of the longer letters.

The central climax of these letters is the events surrounding the Battle of Messines 1914, and the actual battle itself, which essentially was the 12 day battle for Whyschate village and the Messines ridge above it.

BACKGROUND

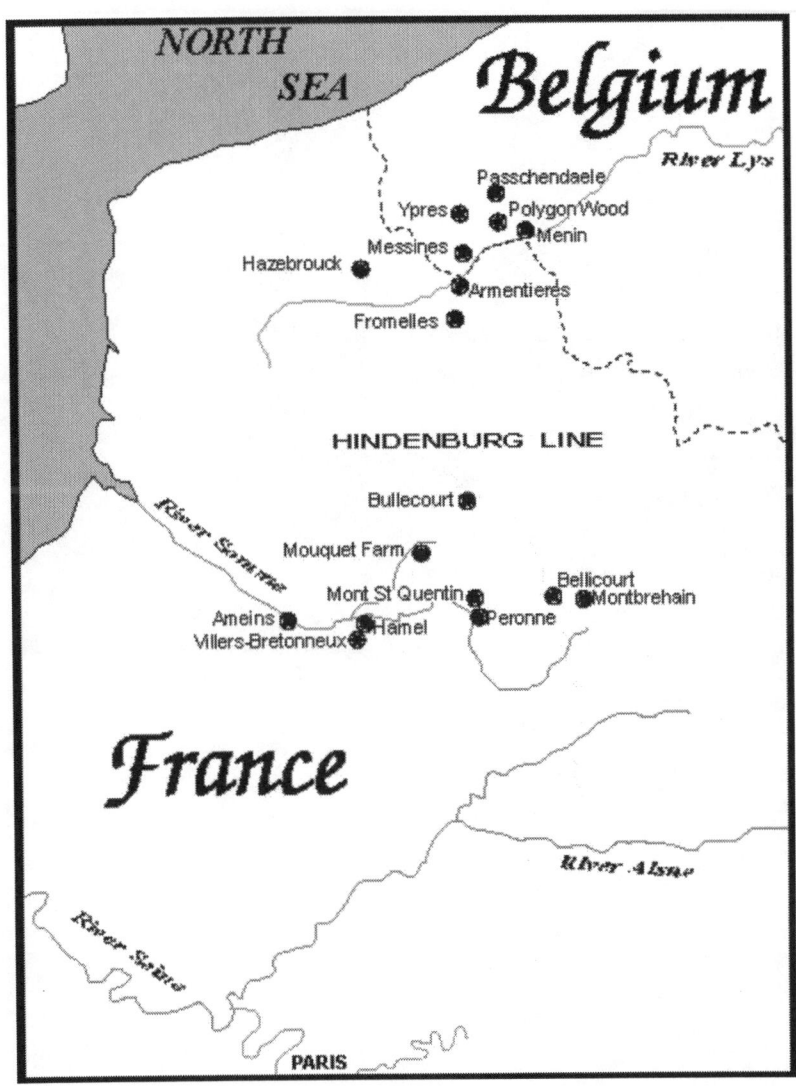

THE BATTLE

The battle was part of the First Battle of Ypres, which is usually dated as 12th October to 22nd November 1914. There are two key phases –the initial German advance and then the subsequent defence. In the big picture Ypres represents the salient to be held at all costs. Even though there were two more battles to come in the area in 1915 and 1917, this first battle has remarkable significance for all the sides involved. The Belgiums were overrun here. The French took remarkable casualties. For the British, "Wipers" will forever tug at the heart. And for the Germans this battle became known as the Kindermond ("slaughter of the innocents"), with Langemarck being their memorial ground.

"Peach" a mans man during the retreat

Flanders has long been a corridor of conflict. It is a level plain with a slight hill rising 200 ft at Kemmel, and 100 foot ridges at Wytschaete, Gheluvelt and Passchendaele. The area was heavy clay, with a high water table. The locations named are mostly large villages, or small towns. Wytschaete had a population of only 3,500, Messines 1,400 and even Ypres just 17,000. The weather was fine during the battle, although there was heavy rain on two days in November, and the area froze up towards the end of November. The battle had followed the battle of Mons in August, and the Marne and the Aisne in September. These battles had ended in immobile deadlock and so there was a race to get around this scene. The race to the sea.

The fighting began in earnest in mid October. The British had had warning of it from wireless intercepts. In addition there were the artillery bombardments that preceded the attacks – already a common feature by this time. But they underestimated the scale. Smith Dorrien, the General in charge of the Messines sector at the time wrote at the time

> *"I honestly do not see how the war can be a very long one – and still believe I shall be walking round the garden with my Dear, looking at the borders and hoping the pet one will really come out all blue, before the Daffodils have ceased to flower."*

The British withdrew after first contact to the ridge on the east of Messines village and were ordered to dig in. They lost and retook this position several times and the confused fighting ended in the inevitable stalemate that came to characterise the next four years. If only they had known it then! By mid November they were pushed off the ridge, but fell back a mile or so to consolidate on the west side of Messines village. Both sides tried to make themselves comfortable for the winter ahead during the intense cold that came in late November and the attacks were called off. It was a conscious throwback to the seasonal Peninsular wars of a hundred years before.

The Germans had had overwhelming numbers but they overestimated their enemy, just as the British had underestimated the Germans. This misinformation and lack of communication with the front would also feature throughout this war, and never again.

On the day Falkenhayn issued orders for the offensive, General French reported to Kitchener that the Germans

> *"were quite incapable of making any strong and sustained attack."*

By 31st October, Wytschaete was held by just 415 men from the Household Cavalry and just 600 men held the Messines ridge. Facing them was 12 times that number - six German Battalions.

Sir John French had gone that day by car to visit Haig. He had to drive through Ypres and met a white faced Haig pouring over maps with John Gough, on dining room table at the Hooge Chateau.

> *"They have broken us right in and are pouring through the gap"*

French recorded this in his memoirs as his worst half hour

> *"in a life full of vicissitudes".*

And Pedlar, who was with him although not on that day called it "his blackest day".

French had seen what he called

> *"full retreat on Ypres…There is nothing left for me to do but go up and be killed with 1st Corps."*

They were talking about the fall of Gheluvelt, the last defensive line a few miles east of Ypres. In fact as they were talking it had just been retaken. On that day the Worcester Regiment had their

THE BATTLE

most famous day of all and retook Gheluvelt in a dramatic charge. But lack of communication with the front dominated this war.

Just after midnight hours on the following day, 1st November, Foch, in charge of the whole combined allied forces, visited GHQ at St Omer. He met General French in his night shirt. According to Foch, French was in a panic.

"We are for it!" said French.

"We shall see", replied Foch, *"In the meantime, hammer away, hammer away, keep on hammering, and you will get there."*

Other accounts – all of them from Francophile sources have Foch saying

"We must stand firm first, we can die afterwards"

And

"you must not talk of dying, but of winning"

and in another report

"Marshall your lines are pierced. You have no troops available. You are finished. Then you must advance. If you retreat voluntarily, you will be swept up like straws in the gale."

French merely wrote:

"we all went thoroughly into the situation"

Although pushed back by the mass German attack the British held their line. A junior officer Duncan Balfour recorded in his diary

> *"we came out and lined the filed for about fifteen minutes potting away at them.*
> *They were coming up in line, about four paces between each man,*
> *but line after line like a piece of paper that had been ruled out."*

Had the Germans known it, there was little behind the front, and almost no one to protect the headquarters. At one time, as Pedlar relates, cooks and household-mess staff at headquarters were press-ganged to arms on the 31st October. One German officer was captured at Nonnebosschen wood. He asked where the British reserves were. According to I.Mowbray, the British officer pointed to a line on the horizon. He was pressed to say what the line actually was. When told it was headquarters the German officer's jaw dropped

"Gott Almighty!"

The Germans had failed to consolidate their attacks. They tried too many points around Ypres and consistently overestimated the scattered rifle fire facing them. And when they did overwhelm that fire it appeared that they equally imagined those same main lines to be just outposts of the front line. No great reserves stood behind these British regiments.

The Germans decided to abandon the offensive on 17th No-

THE BATTLE

vember, although sporadic fighting continued on throughout November. Albrecht, supported by Falkenhayn, took the decision. Falkenhayn had refused to send more men from other theatres of war to concentrate on this sector. The weather had turned with serious frost on the 15th, and heavy snow must have been forecast, and indeed followed on the 19th.

When the Germans called off the attack at the end of November the British were finished. Sergeant John Lucy of the 2nd Royal Irish Rifles commented on his colleagues coming to join him at the front,

> *"shiftless, half-baked in every way, and the non-commissioned officers were very poor stuff...*
> *The old army was finished."*

The British official history put it like this

> *"The line that stood between the British Empire and ruin was composed of tired, haggard and unshaven men, unwashed, plastered with mud, many in little more than rags."*

And Pedlar, as these letters show, talked of the few hundred men holding the ten miles between Messines and Ypres.

HITLER'S PART IN THE BATTLE

Hitler kept a painting he had made during this conflict of Messines chapel in his office for the remainder of his life. He had been a struggling young artist in Munich having left Austria in 1912 to avoid conscription. When war came he signed up. He went for immediate training in August 1914 and his regiment the 16th Bavarians were sent by train to Lille in October. From there they marched to the front to Gheluvelt, a few miles east of Ypres. They took enormous losses, with 350 men of his regiment killed fighting in that area on the first day alone. However by November they had the upper hand south of Gheluvelt and were pushing the British off the Messines Ridge. He wrote to his landlord

> *"we were all proud of having licked the Britishers. Since then we have been in the front lines the whole time. I was proposed for the Iron Cross!"*

While the decoration was being given to Hitler he and three others were asked to step outside the bunker. Just as he did so a British shell landed on the roof, killing or wounding all those inside.

Hitler was promoted and given a job as "Meldeganger" or dispatch runner, with Corporal rank. He painted the scenes at Messines and wrote again to his landlord

> *"Our regiment has been constantly in the front line between Messines and Wytschaete. The meadows and the files look like bottomless swamps, while the roads are covered ankle deep in mud. Through these swamps run the trenches of our infantry, a maze of dug-outs and trenches with loopholes. The air has been trembling under the*

screams and roars or grenades and the bursting of shells. What is most dreadful is when the guns begin to spit across the whole front at night... nothing is ever going to shift us from here. "

A colleague of his called Mend wrote in 1931 how Hitler

"Made long muddled speeches to the men...and made little clay figures, stood them in a row on the parapet and harangued them about how, after the war was won, social order would be changed and a new order set up. More and more is comrades came to look on him as an absurd braggart and a crazy chatterbox whom no one could take seriously."

Mend was summoned by the Gestapo soon after and was never seen again.

Hitler created the Myth of Langemarck referred to above. It is a village just 10 miles north east of Ypres and not strictly the exact battlefield, although German cemeteries are there. He wrote

"From the distance the strains of a song reached our ears, coming closer and closer, leaping from company to company , and just as death plunged a busy hand into our ranks, the song reached us too and we passed it along. "Deutscheland, Deutscheland uber Alles"

Later sources say that the Germans sung to help with identity for those not wearing the pickelhaube helmet. Whatever the truth, it gives a vivid picture of the fighting at the time, much of which, as we shall see, was hand to hand with bayonets in trenches.

SIGNIFICANCE OF THE FIRST BATTLE OF YPRES

Hindsight shows that the battle was every bit as important as Pedlar warned at the time. The German Chief of Staff Erich von Falkenhayn reasoned shortly after the battle and again in his memoirs that there was no more possibility for Germany to win the war. The defensive trenches beat back the offensive push by the Germans. Lightly armed Cavalry like the 12th Lancers jumped into the trenches and proved able to hold off mass attacks by enemy formations backed by artillery. As we learn here, at the time that the Germans called off the assault just a few hundred men remained holding miles of front that had been the point of the entire German Army just days before. The Allied success was defensive, not offensive and this set the tone for the next four years.

Mont des cats R.H.A. being shelling

This fact had a profound effect on the emerging Douglas Haig. Haig became the Commander in Chief of the British Army over a year later in December 1915. He now knew that the Germans had called off their offensive too early. He knew that really the British had been beaten and that the Germans had missed their chance. During the Third Battle of Ypres three years later, Haig made references to the events of the first battle in 1914,

SIGNIFICANCE OF THE FIRST BATTLE OF YPRES

"We must not make the same error"

He was determined not to repeat the mistake when and if he had the chance to get on the offensive again. He by then understood this to be a war of attrition and that victory would therefore belong to the side that stuck it out to survive.

The First Battle of Ypres marked the end of the British Expeditionary Force BEF.

"The Old Comtemptibles".

The British casualties for the 42 days of 14 October – 30 November are usually reported at an astonishing 58,155, close to the size of the entire standing British Army today, and most of the 80,000 initially sent out to fight as the British Expeditionary Force BEF. This professional elite had trained in the Boer War and "in the Grim" on Kipling's North West Frontier but was wiped clean away. Although it came back as a new volunteer army the decimation of the veterans was complete.

Those numbers do not match the French casualties. Fighting on the right flank of the British they took losses of 86,237. The offensive Germans took losses to match the other two combined, weighing in at a jaw dropping 134,315. No wonder they called it off. Nothing like these numbers had ever been seen before in world history.

There were other "firsts" at this time. This was the first battle in history that was recorded in letters home that were delivered within 48 hours, and sometimes sent twice per day. This communication was a first, but the dominance of the artillery conversely restricted the Generals' communication with the front for the first time. These letters reveal that the 12 Lancers were cut off from the rest of the army for days at a time without communication or supplies, and fought on regardless. The lack of real time information flows also fooled the German Generals. Staff officers massively overestimated in their reports the numbers facing them at the time that they called off the battle. But no factual histories nor casualty numbers convey feeling like these letters.

Oosteverne - Where cavalry dug trenches for the first time

SIGNIFICANCE OF THE FIRST BATTLE OF YPRES

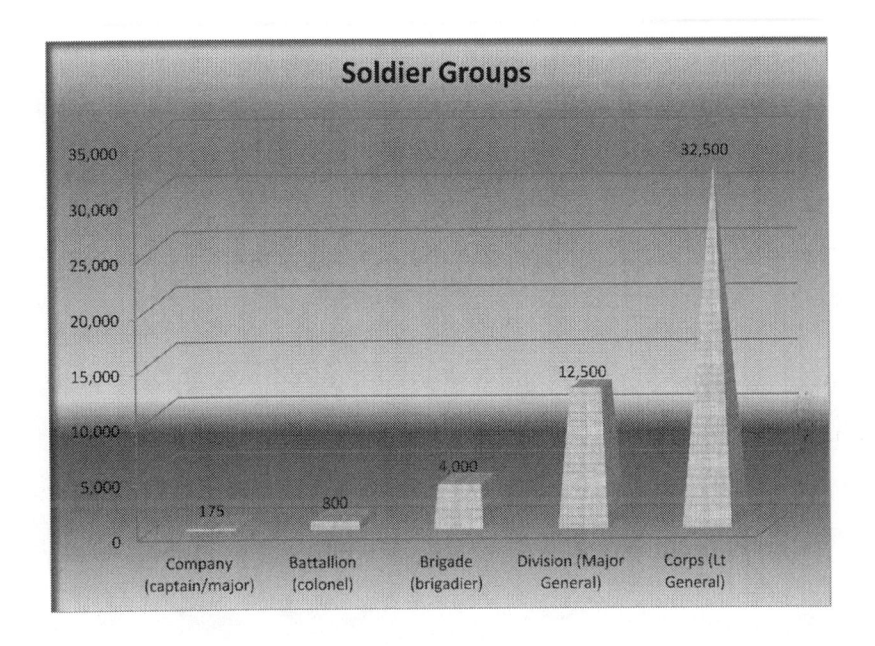

Soldier Groups

Unit	Size
Company (captain/major)	175
Battallion (colonel)	300
Brigade (brigadier)	4,000
Division (Major General)	12,500
Corps (Lt General)	32,500

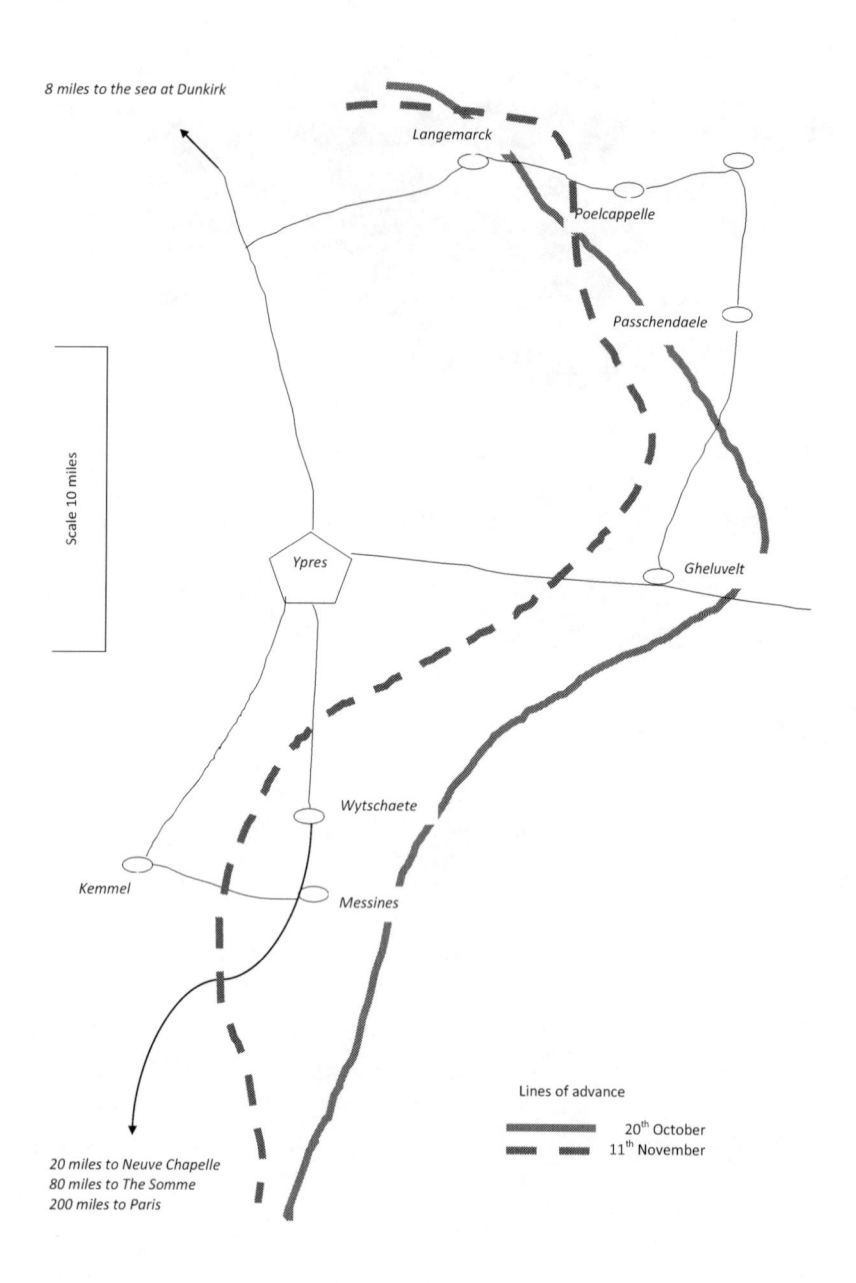

LETTERS FROM THE FRONT

8 miles to the sea at Dunkirk

Langemarck

Poelcappelle

Passchendaele

Scale 10 miles

Ypres

Gheluvelt

Wytschaete

Kemmel Messines

Lines of advance

— 20th October
- - - 11th November

20 miles to Neuve Chapelle
80 miles to The Somme
200 miles to Paris

THE CHARM OF THE LETTERS

Pedlar writes with emotion, but also has sufficient wit to understand the importance of his war during these few months. We can also be grateful that he lacked the tact that soften later letters not published here. He did not spare his wife.

> *"...Kill or be killed"*

> *"...Covered in German blood"*

and

> *"...I may be killed any moment"*

are lines from within. This was him. We can be sure of this because when his young brother in law Bob Wendover died of gangrenous wounds in 1916 Pedlar recounted the truth of his suffering to the sisters. One of the sister's children, Elizabeth Basset, wrote in her autobiography 80 years later

> *"I found it hard to forgive Uncle Pedlar for repeating this..."*

He tended towards tactless and this makes the letters even more reliable a source of real feeling.

Although there are letters from Pedlar to his wife for all his time in war through 1915 and 1916 until he was wounded on the Somme they are not published here. The later letters do contain a few snappy stories from Pedlar's daily life recounted as gossip.

A junior sentry shoots a senior officer dead for not answering the code correctly.

A chauffeur is killed by a shell as the Prince of Wales clambers out of his car.

Nineteen officers join him at an impromptu "bring your own" party in the front line.

But these later letters are different. They are written after he had seen the readers of his first letters, and discussed the contents with them. He discovered a gulf in understanding

"I never realised war was like this"

he says in his second letter, and surely this realisation can never be communicated to a non-combatant. Later letters lack urgency and naïveté. They contain general themes, less detail, and give unconvincing reassurance for the mother of his children

Pedlar, Howes, Forman, Ebrington, Chetwode, Walwyn, Maxwell

THE CHARM OF THE LETTERS

5th Cavalry brigade en route to Houve - France

"I fear nothing in this war. I have no qualms at all...Don't worry about the papers,
I am not in it in any way whatsoever. I should tell you if I were, or even likely to be".

Compare those empty platitudes with

"this is so awful, all my friends are dead"

From the November 3rd 1914 letter. In short after Pedlar had met with his readership and heard some feedback in early 1915 he began to write for his audience. I think he realised in 1914 that his audience would be reading the letters years later. He understood the enormity of it all.

The letters were sent to any one of four addresses, and when wrong they were forwarded on to one of the other three addresses. These addresses were Daws Hill, High Wycombe, which was The Marquis of Lincolnshire's house, Old Mill Cottage, High Wycombe and 53 Princes Gate and 13 Queens Gate, both in west London. This tracks the movement of his wife and two young children between her family addresses at the time.

All text in (brackets) has been added by the editor to avoid distracting footnotes.

27th AUGUST 1914
First letter from France - with section cut out by censors

My beloved Angel,

The crisis approaches very rapidly – we shall have a desperate encounter and after that I hope an end.

We have been marching for five days in retreat – trying to draw the Germans onto us. We have had a lot of little scraps with my brigade, and we have always done very well so far.

It really is a dreadful sight to see all the women and children flying from the villages and towns. It really is too awful and is to my mind the worst side of the whole thing.

Refugees fled wearing their "sunday best" cloths

It is horribly tiring. We are always on the move at 3.30am and I never finish until 11.30pm. However weather is glorious and I am very well and comparatively fit. But oh, how I long to end it all and be back with my darling again, but it is not to be. I have had quite a number of letters from you but nothing else, it is very nice hearing occasionally.

I like my guard very much and think him a genuine good man. The

Coldstream did awfully well in a bayonet charge in the streets. They put up a magnificent fight.

There is so much to say, it is very hot and if over tired our fellows cannot do themselves justice. I do hope the babes are enjoying their London season.

Pedlar.

Howes, Pedlar, Sir P Chetwode, Col Buckely Johnson, RS Gregs. Just before the batlle of Ypres

5th SEPTEMBER
"I never realised war was like this"

My darling beloved,

How awful it must be for you all this time. But I hope you have enough to do to keep your mind occupied. We have a hard time. We move at 3.30 or 4am daily and never get in until after dark. It is very tiring and all night I have to prepare returns and reports of all kinds. It is very tiring work and I seldom get sleep of more than 2 or 3 hours. We are on the move all day doing flank or rear guards to the 1st Army Corps (Douglas Haig) which entails long arduous halt, we move from sky line to skyline. We usually have a daily scrap with patrols or small parties, but we have been making one long retirement in the face of overwhelming numbers. I fancy we shall soon turn around and fight.

We have had quite a lot of casualties and we are always losing two or three men at a time. This war is at terrible high pressure – everyone's nerves are highly tired, the physical fatigue and mental strain of very rapid movements is very taxing. I have seen a great deal of General Haig and his chief of staff John Gough, (General Sir John) as I am always going with despatches. They are both very cool and very confident although they fear the heat affect upon our infantry.

At Kemmel - Williams by a shell hole

There are lots of things I must tell you, but we are so very busy that I omit them. The irregularity of my life is rather trying but I manage to keep my bowels open by diet of fruits. I am very uncomfortable – none of my kit is what I wanted my servants are very bad and I have no time to arrange things in order. I have my washing case, and one change of clothing. My General (Sir Philip Chetwode) has lost all his kit and has absolutely nothing except what he stands in, which is really very trying for him.

He is a marvellous man with a Napoleonic conception of war and I consider a very great leader. He and Hubert Gough stand out as commanders.

The Guards Brigade 4th had a good fight in the forest of Villers Cutteret. (just north of Paris) Colonel Morris was killed and many wounded they fought very well and inflicted tremendous losses on the enemy. We were there, but unable to act in the forest.

Our infantry have been marched to a standstill. They had to withdraw from a nasty salient which became very precarious owing to the failure of the French to keep back a certain German corps. Therefore we had to race back to a line more strategically sound that had the advanced position in Belgium. More, I am not allowed to state.

We shall have a great battle within a few days as we are all massed ready for immediate action. I would like you to see Dad and Allen (elder brother) about my horses. I am afraid "Brandy" is with the yeomanry, but provided they note him down I can buy him back after the war. Comet must not go. Let me know what has happened to all my horses and ponies. I saw Nobby one day, looking very fit and well, is full of cheer I hope all of you are well at home. I see Bob (his wife's young brother, Lord Bob Wendover, aged just 18) has been gazetted and let's hope he will not have to come out here. It will be a great disaster if we are beaten by these Germans but I think not.

I never realised war was so hard – never has a war been conducted at such a great pace or at such never ending relentlessness.

Approach March towards Mons - Brigade massing in the open

4th SEPTEMBER
General Chetwode's great work

My darling beloved,

Yesterday we had a bad day – and I have already written a long letter to Mummy and I will not repeat myself to you because it depresses me. We have had to reform the cavalry owing to the arrival of new corps. We are now incorporated into the 2nd Cavalry Division and our glorious brigade has come to an end. It is unfortunate because we have done so well as a brigade and are now no longer independent.

1st battle of Ypres - Zandvoorde after shell fire

We have had a very trying time of late – breakfast 4.30am does not suit me, with only a sandwich until 8pm. I have had a tremendous lot of work and have so far been successful in feeding my brigade without mishap. A unique feat as no other brigade cavalry or infantry has had its food regularly. We are a very happy home, the greys and 12th and we are by a long way the finest cavalry brigade. The greys are splendid. I eat whatever I can lay hands on at breakfast, usually a bit of bacon and bread and jam. Sometimes only bread and cheese. Then a cheese sandwich or ration biscuit for sandwich and dinner always the same – a chick and tons of vegetables. We usually sleep on a bundle of straw, three or four of us

4TH SEPTEMBER

in a heap.

Your comforts are a great boon to me especially this writing pad, shall want refills for it soon. I am really very fit and well, and under the circumstances am as happy as any man. Our troops one marvels and in my opinion esprit de corps is worth 6 to 1. The good regiments are very valuable. The guards are real good. There is no doubt that a man well bred and well brought up stands out as a leader of men in an emergency. I wrote to you yesterday (letter above) when I thought one might be bowled over at any moment. We had the most trying day I ever have experienced. To see glorious men shot down by tens without rhyme or response was enough to sicken a man of war forever.

Will you write to Lady Chetwode (wife of General in Command) and tell her how proud we all are of her husband. The men love him and the officers realise that he is a great soldier. He has covered himself in the glory – not only in making a new formation into the finest brigade of our cavalry, but in gaining successes of momentous importance when a reverse would have been calamity. His power of concentration his quickness of decision his loyalty to his staff and his officers have enabled him to achieve success and I am sure to earn well merited reward for his work for the worlds future history.

I hope the children are enjoying London, and not becoming pale and unfit. Poor Sam, the retriever. I hope is in London with them. I hope so.

Yours Pedlar.

14th SEPTEMBER

Not sent until 14th November, see letter of that day. On a scrap of paper, in pencil and almost inelegible

To my wife,

14/9/14

1.5.am

Vailly

To my beloved darling,

God knows my love for you knows no equal.

Your loving heart must be heavy today I am in a rather dangerous place and may be killed at any moment.

God bless you from your

Pedlar.

Kemmel Tower - twice hit

Eusty, Pedlar, Edwards, Jacky darling midday rest after 3 30am rendezvous - villenauve sous thery

16th SEPTEMBER
Eustace Crawley going well

Darling Beloved,

Today is a day of quiet, because we had an awful time two days ago, and since then the battle has raged between infantry and Artillery – The Guards Brigade of the 1st Division fought a great contest last night, one of a hundred phases of this enormous battle. They were very heavily counter attacked by masses of gunners and became sick of the human slaughter for the Germans sent column after column. Finally the Guards repelled the counter attack with great loss and the day (15th) closed with troops stationery and utterly exhausted.

I have broken the electric torch which you sent me although I still *have the battery I brought in Wilkinson's No 800 B.S. of which I send a mark. It would be nice to receive a weekly refill for it.*

There is an enormous battle raging now and the boom of the guns becomes monotonous.

I am very anxious to know about the 10th(Hussars) I wonder if you know anything?

The general is a tapper, and keeps us all hard at work.

I got the Times of the 5th today and now I receive your letters quite regularly which is a great joy. Eustace Crawley is in great form and is always very cheery. I hope you are not to dreadfully dull in London, I hope you see all your friends and keep your spirits up. Mind you take plenty of exercise.

THE FIGHT FOR WYSCHATE AND THE BATTLE OF MESSINES

The Great German offensive was launched on 19th October.

23rd OCTOBER
Goodbye to the horses

Darling Beloved,

Pass this onto Dad and Mother please

Grave of an unkown soldier

The 2nd Cavalry division are now in trenches between 2 army corps. Let me give you an idea of the work

We had been on a prototype cavalry mission. When we received orders to go to a certain line and there link up with and continue the line of an army corps. This we did four nights ago – dug trenches with bayonets, and said goodbye to our horses.

We still continue to hold the line.

Yesterday another corps came on our left, and the cavalry corps now occupies seven miles of front.

Last night at dusk 5.15pm a very heavy attack developed on our left. The brigade on our left fell back to a more secure line.

We had to conform, but as soon as we moved the Germans came on and things began to look rather serious, especially as we fell back to open ground leaving our trenches to the enemy. The order therefore was given to re-gain the trenches with bayonet. We had 1,000 yards at least to cover before we got back to where we were before.

It did not take long to get back. Whatever happened I don't know, but as soon as we went back to retake our trenches the Germans were off and we regained the trenches with comparatively little loss of life. Time 6pm dark.

Pedlar

Then we began preparing for a counter attack. At 8pm the Germans opened with a gun 450 yards from our trenches, and the men in the trenches could distinctly hear the infantry words of command as patrols reported large forward bodies massing in the valley.

All night they waited further onslaught. It came at 4am. Such a thun-

23RD OCTOBER

der of shrapnel, shell and shot. In a few moments many farms and one town were alight. Their fire caused a weird and lurid affect amidst the deafening roar.

But our men stuck it out, and as usual the Germans failed to come to grips, our men are used to shrapnel and just drop down in the trenches when the storm of shrapnel comes.

So here we daring infantry, but without any of the means at ones disposal that they have. We dug trenches with our finger nails and bayonets, with pitchforks and I saw one man using a coal shuttle!!

We have no supports or reserves like infantry, no reliefs of men or officers.

This was the fourth day, and the officers to a man have had no sleep night and day – certainly not at night. All the men are stone cold with physical aches. As men they are without support or reserves and every rifle has to be used.

Bulge "a glorious man" killed leading Welsh guards at Loos

The German losses are terrible. In front of our 12th Infantry Brigade

49

this morning they picked up 801 dead Germans!! Think of it. It's appalling.

We have had enough of treachery and deceit. There is no quarter. When our men get to close quarters, he kills or is killed.

Yesterday one line of Germans saw our men advancing with bayonet. And to save themselves they stood up in their trenches and hurled down their rifles to the ground. We hope their lives were spared, but perhaps they paid for the treachery of others. In these conflicts there is such a holocaust of death that there is no time for questions.

The first Corps (Haig) fired 1,800 rounds at 1,000 yards range into masses of Germans, and you can imagine the awful carnage.

We are now spending our fourth night in the trenches, and have been attacked all day. At dusk a company of Sikhs came up to let one of our squadrons have a rest. At this stage of the campaign the squadrons are very weak and a squadron can only put a maximum of 20 rifles into firing line because of led horses and all that. There is no error about this game – we see the Germans massing against us and simply wait all night to know which position of our little thin line has to bear the brunt of the assault.

French Zouaves. 1st battle of Ypres

23RD OCTOBER

A curious role for cavalry, talk of the honour of infantry in trenches!

Here are we no supports or reserves – no sleep - no one who knows how to even dig a trench – no method of feeding the men in the trenches.

Yet for <u>four days and nights</u> we have been under a ceaseless shrapnel and rifle fire, and have actually counter attacked the German infantry and driven them off. <u>Four days and four nights without a break.</u>

Such is war. But our men are glorious and will never acknowledge defeat whilst the blood still runs in their veins.

The people of England should be made to realise the uselessness of sending out new units. It is violating every principle and is courting disaster, to send units improvised and poorly officered.

Let sections of infantry or Troops of cavalry be sent to fill the gaps in the existing forces. Thereby backbone is assured as the new ones will soon shake down amongst the seasoned men. The units here will be invigorated by arrival of fresh blood. Conversely the fresh arrivals will assimilate their new conditions very quickly.

Any other method is short sighted. Commanders of all units of all arms realise that what is wanted is not a figurative army, but they require solid drafts to fill up the vacancies.

Let those drafts be under an officer who KNOWS his men – who has trained them even for a few weeks in England. Then these men will be able to do themselves justice and do credit to the regiment to which they are sent.

Any other idea of raising regiments and officering with inexperienced officers is to court disaster.

The Northumberland Yeomanry are very good – all farmers and glorious men, and they know their officers and the secret of men.

When one sees death being dealt out by shrapnel- shell and bullet, small wonder that the men rely on their officers for help. Small wonder that he who fails to lead his men correctly fails and will never regain the confidence of his men.

You can publish any of this.

Bless you my darling,

Yours Pedlar.

Kemmel Billet

23rd OCTOBER
Card

Dearest, Dreadfully fatiguing work night and day in trenches and this one 7th day, without relief! Every night we have at least two, sometimes four attacks, guns-rifles, we usually have an attack at dawn.

All well best love, Pedlar

Dearest,

Dreadfully fatiguing work night & day in trenches and this our 7th day, without relief!! Every night we have at least 2, sometimes 4 attacks. Guns - rifles - maxims - usually have an attack at dawn.

All well, best love

Pallan

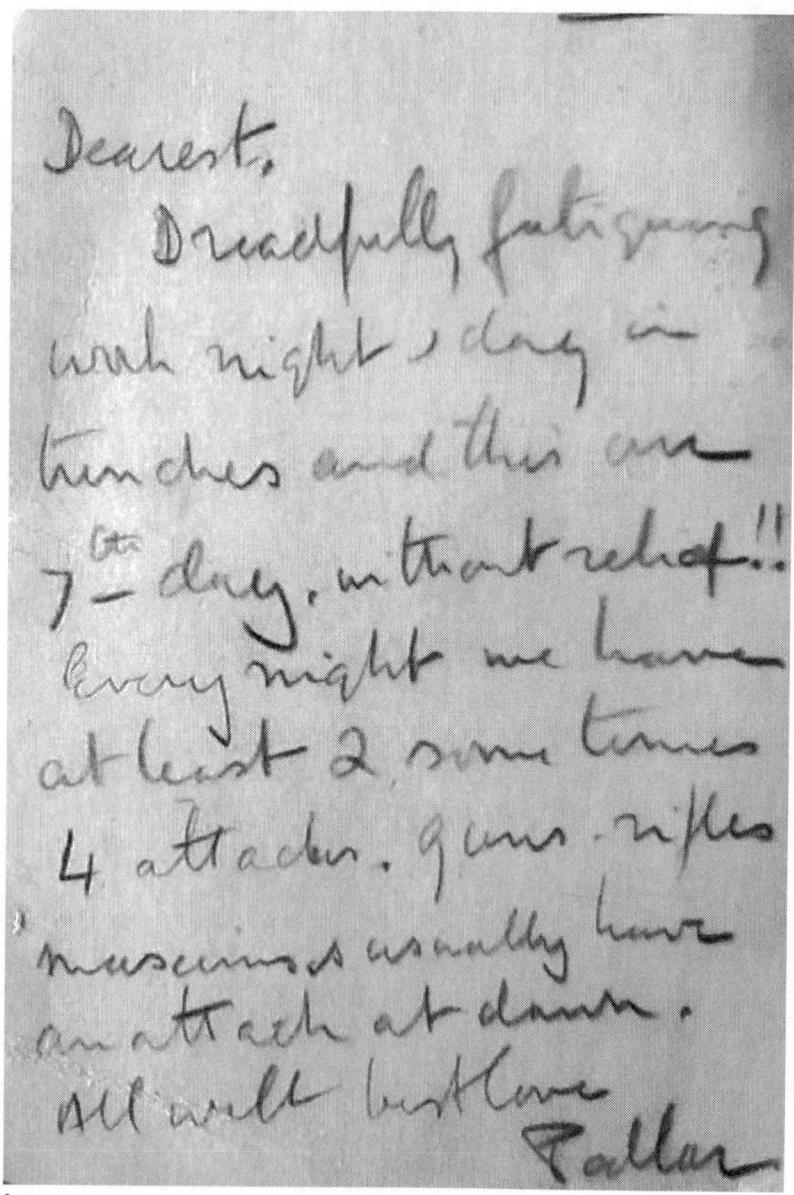

Letter

3rd NOVEMBER
Covered from head to foot in German blood

My precious Darling

What we have been through for these last 10 days is beyond my power to describe. No troops in the world have ever done what our cavalry have done. Night and day in the trenches with at least four or five attacks every night.

Finally we were driven in by an enormous mass of Germans. One German corps attacked one cavalry brigade = 800 rifles in the trenches!! The carabineers were walked over and literally buried in their trenches by masses of Germans. Line after line. (Beckett 2004 says 415 British versus six German Brigades, "odds of 12:1 against".)

One town was taken and retaken three times during the night. I was with the 12th Lancers all night lying 200 yards from that town. The Lincoln's fought like heroes all night in this town – losing half its men. All night long we lay watching the burning town and the awful conflict. At daybreak we saw some Germans coming towards us. This was too much for the men of the 12th who rose up to a man and gave such ringing cheers that Germans thought an army corps was on them. They jumped out of windows and houses and ran everywhere but the boys of the 12th formed a line and at a run with fixed bayonets they cleaned the streets of the town – killing every man they saw – no quarter – no captures. The men were mad. They hunted the Germans down like chickens using the butts of their rifles. They charged right on through the town and we saw the Germans in full flight over the valley. Never have I seen men so mad.

LETTERS FROM THE FRONT

Puggy Howes, Bulger Williams, "Wombat" Howard Lyse, G.O.C. Sir Philip Chetwode, Pedlar. Note - ever present open map

A wonderful thing to see these cavalry men charging like the best of infantry. Everyman killed at least three Germans. One officer killed 11, and was covered in German blood from head to foot.

I did not kill any – I was conducting the operation under my Generals orders and was very tired and as soon as the danger was over I sat and watched the slaughter with absolute joy.

Poor (Major) Eustace Crawley was killed by a shell today – he was sitting in a trench between two others and a shell blew his head off.

Darling this is awful – all my friends are being killed.

Pedlar with Eustace Crawley in Madras

56

3RD NOVEMBER

The hand of god guides me and one's life is solely in God's keeping.

No one can realise what this war is unless he has seen it.

God bless you,

Pedlar.

5th NOVEMBER
Five days and nights without sleep

My darling Beloved,

The terrible contest still continues. The cavalry has performed deeds of heroism which baffle description.

For five days and five nights a German corps assaulted the trenches held by one cavalry division = 9 regiments = 1,300 riles!

The Carabineers were absolutely walked over by one dense column – but never a man left his trench indeed he couldn't for the Germans were walking on his head as the bodies of dead. This same column swept on to attack a town and in two hours came back over the Carabineers who turned round in their trenches to meet it. But as soon as the foremost Germans impaled themselves on the bayonets the masses behind bore friends and foe to the ground and surged on to its objective.

Our horse artillery guns were behind us night and day and at night the roar of the artillery guns was terrible. The rapidity of the fire is much more demoralising than the explosion of the largest shell.

The Germans turned their big guns onto our trenches and in places our trenches were literally blown out of the ground by these "Black Marias". For 12 days our little thin line was assaulted by a whole German Corps. As our orders laconically recorded. "No further corps have arrived in our front". Well its over now and the French have taken up our line. The French regards us as heroes and history will

5TH NOVEMBER

reveal the splendid action of the British Cavalry.

I hope people are gradually realising that the army has been re-manned ie 100 per cent losses have been sustained already. General Allenby and even Sir John French are doing their utmost to prevent Brigades of yeomanry coming out – because it is slaughter. However the political pressure is great and they say it is good for recruiting! Can it be time that enough recruits are forthcoming. Can it be true that our men of Yorkshire and Lancashire do not realise what happened to their fellow mates in the valley of the Sambe. Lille Liege, Charleroi Etc = the black country of England.

I don't believe our masses realise it and never will until they have seen their homes burnt, their women and children driven in hordes like cattle along a road, swept here and there as the fortunes of war fluctuate. The men of England would be as bad a soldier as the German were it not for the British Officer.

The officers make and mould their men and the officers can make men of moderate quality perform deeds of valour without officers our little army would be useless – even the most youthful boy of 18 rises to the occasion and commands the complete confidence of his men where an experienced NCO has failed. Such is the unquestionable law of personality and power of command.

The Germans have failed in their attempt to terrorise England by a seizure of Calais. Kaiser Wilhelm billeted in a chateau within range of our guns, in his mad efforts to crush our army. He hurled corps after corps at our army, only to personally witness the mangled remains recoiling from the invincibles.

The Navy has a difficult task for if the Germans gain a sea front they will transport submarines and light craft by train and play havoc.

But naval wars are always indecisive, no naval war has ever yet brought war to an end or even near it. When Russia invades Silesia we shall hear the shrieks of the German nation. As it suddenly realises the truth. I have written a post card for a haversack made by Winder of Conduit Street. Also I want a lamp made by Stewart of Strand. Called Rolux I think). No other is of any use.

God bless you my darling angel.

I loved the photos of the kids and have written to Sybil.

Yours Pedlar.

Battle scene - After rout of Germains at Gandaleu

6th NOVEMBER
14 days holding the lines

Darling Andyriggs.

Your letter about Sir Frank made me very sad. Poor woman. Nothing one can do can alleviate her sorrow.

Three french officers - Chasseurs

Well we have beaten them. The great mass was hurled at us led by Kaiser in person has been sent back stunned decimated and routed. The first corps bore the brunt of it. We cavalrymen have performed deeds of which even I did not think our men capable. We have for 14 days held a line which is now being held by 2 French corps!! We hurled back attack after attack and frustrated the attempt to break us. Had we gone or been beaten we should have caused the British army a great defeat. Because the 1st Corps would have been surrounded. Our losses baffle description or even belief. 212 officers, 2,300 men have paid for this. The 9th Lancers have 7 officers and 117 men. The 4th Dragoon Guards 5 officers and 93 men. Our men fought like demons, and would not leave their trenches, even though the Germans blew portions off those trenches to pieces by high explosive shell. Our cavalry ceases to exist. But we shall gradually re-organise and slowly re-officer.

Harry Crichton behaved heroically. He was in command of a regiment some of which gave way - I am sorry to say - but Crichton tried to stop them but was caught by the Germans, but I don't think he was killed. (Viscount Henry Crichton was actually killed aged 42, leaving a 7 year old son, who later became 5th Earl Erne).

1. Captain "Rolly" Charrington, 2. Captain Reggie Badger, 3. French Interpreter, 4. Captain Richard Howard Vyse, 5. Brigadier General Sir Philip Chetwode, 6. Major Eustace Crawley, 7. Pedlar Staff Captain, 8. Captain Charles Bryant. September 1914. Note - sun protection

German prisoners taken 5th cavalry brigade

Curiously enough it was at that very spot the previous night with Bulkeley Johnson of the Blues and I remonstrated with him that I did not think his line of trenches was good enough. They were not placed right, but they had dug them and would not listen to me. Next night the 2nd Life guards gave way. Quite unnecessarily. I had an awful row with my general. Tom Guerney was in command and when they ran away – the 12th Lancers were sent to fill up the gap. I was sent to direct operations and my general gave me a written order to take Gurney and his men back and put them behind the 12th. Well I got so angry with all the lumber officers who were demoralised and also the men, none of whom were badly wounded. They kept on getting the jumps and Tom Guerney kept rushing up in a panic. So I gave him the order to march his men 5 miles to the rear!

He then reported to my General (Chetwode). When my general asked me about it next day. I said "the men had no officers" but he replied "what do you mean, they had four". No, I said, only four demoralised human beings. Then he laughed and said "I wish there were more like you" but you're too hard on officers who are imperfect.

Well I'll write again later today.

God bless you my angel.

Yours pedlar.

Destruction

7th NOVEMBER
A bitter post battle letter

My darling Angel,

We are now resting after the most awful fight that the world has ever seen, our cavalry have saved the British army from utter disaster. There we stood - a long thin line of glorious men, no supports no reserves – no guns except our glorious horse gunners and even they were reduced to three gun batteries instead of six. For our miserable politicians had saved money by refusing to make guns.

There we were, one long line. Infantry have not only supports and reserves in trenches behind them – but guns of every description to pop shells over their heads and break up formed masses of enemy.

Had we been broken, the 1st Corps on the North Ypres the 2nd Corps on the south Ploegstert would have been beaten in detail. Sir John French himself says so. What a price we paid! We won by Esprit de Corps – nothing else – simply sticking it out regiment by regiment for the sake of esprit de corps.

Our mangled remains are now resting. The whole British army stands paralysed at its losses – stands paralysed and unable to reap the advantages of its heroic achievement.

Paralysed because our miserable economists have thought to pamper the public and save money by refusing to keep those reserves and supplies which all military people demanded. However more men are coming but who are they? Volunteers – glorious men and any man

7TH NOVEMBER

who volunteers for certain death as it is a hero.

Do all the millions of idlers in England realise that the safety of England is not her Navy — England's safeguard is the graves of the thousands of her glorious sons, whilst there are men like them in England - The British Empire will never be shaken.

Yes it's these thousands of graves who have saved the British Empire, what will become of their wives and children? The shirkers in England will do nothing as is obvious by the Prince of Wales fund. 5 Million — why it is a scandal — if every idler gave one weeks wages only then that fund alone would spring to 15 millions.

The British Tommy has no equal black white or yellow — yet his human and at moments of great stress his thoughts are these.

"If I go under what happens to my wife to my kiddies — why poor woman she will go to the workhouse or to the streets, Bob and Bill will get my job, my kids will go to an orphanage. Why shouldn't Bob and Bill do a share of it."

Then a British officer rouses him from his reflections and calls upon him to do or die — which Tommy does. Without an equal, without a qualm. I wonder if Tommy's reflections are not horribly true. Alas Andy, my Darling, I fear they are. For a few years the public will give a little of their wealth amassed by the actions of our glorious men. After a few years they will forget. People in England - partly due to want and dangerous ignorance of war partly due to its innumerable large cities - do not realise that had our little army failed to stem the onslaught of German masses that our Navy would be utterly utterly useless in preventing an invasion.

England weeps when she reads the awful losses, but she does not realise for what cause those losses have been made. She does not realise that had her much maligned and ever abused and even despised little army failed, then those men who had maligned, abused despised it would suffer more than ever the wives of the heroes who are now dead. Unless the nation wakes up and shakes itself it will allow the wives and children of the men, who saved the British Empire from ruin, to suffer and undergo the miseries endured by those widowed in south Africa.

People in England talk about the splendid response of Kitchener's army. It reads like a fairy tale. Kitchener's army indeed! When of the manhood comes forward to do its duty the remainder enriching themselves by the actions of the few who have laid down their lives for their country. Splendid response – The words drive me mad – five millions of money to help the wives and children and one million men.

Let the women of England see the French women being herded along a shell swept road, their burning houses behind them – no one knowing where to go – depending upon the soldiers even for a scrap of biscuit for the children – being wafted about like flies in a drought – poor watchers walking in pouring rain from hell to ladies, often lying in heaps to die at the roadside of sheer despair and starvation.

There will be many volunteers now, but they will simply come to be sacrificed at the expense of, and for the benefit of those in England who have refused to pay for the means of making war, and are now hurling to death thousands of men because they have no the guns

7TH NOVEMBER

which are necessary. Tommy can do and has done much, but there is a limit to human capability.

God bless you my darling.

Your Pedlar.

(1904 to 1914 the British army reduced in size by 16,000 men. ed.)

Whistle

LETTERS FROM THE FRONT

Letter bundle

8th NOVEMBER
From Dranouter, West Flanders

Darling Beloved,

The photo of you and the two boys was splendid. How that young Tony has grown, he looks as big as Peter and what a dear little man he looks. I hope he is as full of mischief as when I last saw him. Keep Peter hard and fit. Plenty of falling about and rough and tumbles. I suppose he is getting to talk a bit now. Do they have meals with you?

Is Missy (sister) living with you now? I hope so as she will feel the first weeks enormously. You look very fine drawn in your photo and I don't like to see you so. Take plenty of walking exercise. Walk with the donkey and keep as fit and well as when we were at Nether Avon. Oh how I wish I was back there.

Here we are all laying down our lives and living in daily peril of great disaster whilst the public at home knows nothing of what is going on. All our officers who return from wounded leave at home – all our men even – say the same awful story.

Those responsible are terrified of revealing the truth for two reasons.

1. *Giving information to the enemy*

2. *Shocking the public by a revelation of the scandalous action of our governments during peace preparation for war.*

They all say that government should on 11th November proclaim national service, together with a very heavy house tax assessed by ratio of males and female occupants. It is sad to think that the British Nation should be unable to realise that some of its men must come forward to do their duty. Soldiers are hired assassins.

Here stands the most glorious little collection of men the world has ever seen – men who for weeks faced the most awful odds, men who for weeks have been deprived of victory because the overwhelming hostile artillery render our own ineffective, men who for weeks have endured the mental strain of seeing their comrades blown to pieces seeing their best efforts nullified (because of the German guns) and endured the physical strain of ceaseless conflict. Here they stand paralysed, because regiments are reduced to companies, batteries to one gun, army corps to brigades. Even the guns they have got have not enough ammunition to allow of correct and adequate use.

These men are the safeguard of England and have already done more to safeguard her shores than would be done by our navy if every single ship was sunk.

Prince Arthur brings dire news

Stir up every man of position in England, every member of parliament, shake him from his coma and make him realise that Government dare not reveal the truth that officers and men are

8TH NOVEMBER

returning in thousands from England to once again do their duty but with hearts saddened by the appalling apathy and ignorance of the great British public. More especially does this apply to the wounded NCOs who are especially saddened by the dangerous carelessness of the masses.

I could say a great deal more, but Kitchener realises the truth, and even he dare not reveal it. Let everyone know what I tell you, what I say now is the reflection of every man of this glorious army, it is more than that, it is the inevitable conclusion arrived at by any man who will dare face facts.

God bless you my beloved

Yours Pedlar.

SUMMARY OF THE BATTLE OF WYTSCHATE 12th NOVEMBER.

The battle of Wytschate

For the 11th day in succession the 12th Lancers were in the trenches when for 11 days and nights they had been been ceaselessly engaged day and night.

A great mass of Germans broke through Messines - 1 ½ divisions against one Battalion of cavalry! (as stated before, odds of 12:1) And late in the night Wytschate fell to the Germans. 2 battalions of English were sent to retake t. The Lincoln's arrived at 2am and attacked, but were unable to make progress. All night long the town reeled with attack and counter attack the cheers of the two forces attacking see attaching.

HQ during the battle of Aisne. Although there are vehicles, roads were rough without tarmac

SUMMARY OF THE BATTLE OF WYTSCHATE

The 12th heard firing from every conceivable direction and lay all night in the trenches awaiting attack. At dawn some Germans were seen by the 12th then the regiment lept from their trenches like one man and with cheers which sent a shiver through one's spine they raced to the Germans. The sound of cheering terrified the Germans who left their position and jumped from the windows of houses etc. But the 12th were at 'em. They bayoneted and struck them down like sheep. In 20 minutes they had cleared the town and stood triumphant watching the Germans running over the valley beyond.

Every man was mad – just blood mad – no German escaped alive they killed 112. And only 178 men of the 12th actually charged.

This game in the trenches is trying. Our line of cavalry has withheld repeated assaults of a German corps and oddments. Every night the roar of musketry and boom of guns at close range kept all men at their posts. Great assaults were delivered but our men were never moved and their deadly fire drove the attacks back.

Finally one night the poor old Blues gave way before stress of numbers, and in other places Carabineers and 9th Lancers the mass of Germans literally buried our little thin line. The Carabineers each had a man on the end of their bayonet – but successive lines of Germans bore them down and friend and foe were hurled into the trenches to be trodden to death by the oncoming hordes.

No infantry in the world – no fanatics in the world have ever fought for 12 days and 12 nights with never an hour of silence. The Germans are regardless of loss of life and select one area and then hurl line after line upon it.

Talk about the value of the infantry at the battle of the Aisne. It was child's play to this battle. In this battle the Germans are trying to break through. We are here to stop them at the Aisne it was an ordinary encounter battle.

The cavalry are decimated, our officers have been sacrificed mercilessly. The death roll bewilders one and one only wonders why I have not been killed yet.

This day we are in reserve as my ears still re-echo with the roar of musketry and guns and one cannot realise that there is silence. Even the French troops hail us with cheers of jubilation wherever we go as sort of heroes. The work of the cavalry corps will live in history to be one of the greatest achievements of the world. More especially since it has been successful.

There is so much to tell you my angel, I cannot write more.

Oh to be with you once more when I come home. We will have a great long honeymoon and you, my life, my all, will just come off with the husband you love so much and we will have a months honeymoon all by ourselves, just you and I, right away from everyone.

All my friends are dead – maimed or dying. My casualty returns nearly break my heart. On one day I had to recall four officers killed, two men killed and seven wounded. The proportion is shocking. Without British officers, even our men would not have stuck it out.

God guard you,

Pedlar.

SUMMARY OF THE BATTLE OF WYTSCHATE

will live in history to be one of the
greatest achievements of the world,
more especially as it has been successful.
There is so much to tell you my angel,
I cannot write more.
Oh to be with you once more —
when I come home — we will have
a great long honeymoon and
you my life, my all, will just
come off with the last band you live in
much, and we will have a months
honeymoon all by ourselves — just
you & I, right away from everyone.
All my friends are dead — maimed, or
dying. My casualty returns nearly break my
heart. On one day I had to recall 40 officers
killed & men killed 7 wounded. The proportion
is shocking. Without officers British officers, even
our men would not have stuck it out.
Godguard you   Pollau

Letter

12th NOVEMBER
723 dead in our trenches

(from Neuve Eglise), 3 miles west of Messines

Darling,

Once again the glorious 1st Corps have performed deeds of heroism which make one proud of the British Soldier. Having tried every corps in the army, Prussia sent for the Imperial Guard corps – we found a copy of its orders which were

> "Men of Imperial Prussian Guard will sacrifice everything in order to break the British and take Ypres. Knapsacks and all accoutrements will be discarded. Rifles only will be taken."

15 Battalions massed against the 1st Infantry Brigade of 1st Corps (strength 4 battalions now totalling at most 1,800 men). 1st Grenadiers, Oxford Light Infantry, Camerons, Shropshires. The German masses were hurled onto these men. All on this little bit of the line, the infantry brigade went back a little, but reformed to counter attack, which it did with such terrible venom that it drove all 15 German battalions clean out and chased them back over their own trenches.

The Germans left 723 dead in <u>our</u> trenches. The prisoners say the shock was terrible for the Germans could not believe our men could survive the weight of numbers. Then I turn to the Times and read the reports

12TH NOVEMBER

Hull "Some inconvenience is being experienced by farmers owing to dearth of labour"

"Some Inconvenience" that's the British public all over, it revolts one to think that such men can call themselves Englishmen. How "inconvenient" people will find it when every Englishman is made to do his duty to his country.

God Bless you,

Yours Pedlar.

Forêt de Saint-Gobain, 5th Cavalry brigade on the move

12th NOVEMBER
Towns deserted and desolate

(From Neuve Eglise)

My precious Angel,

I am very grieved to hear of dear Victoria's loss. (Pedlars sister in Law lost her husband) *Also for Aunt Nora. However let us remember that no Englishman ever laid down his life for a worthier course or for a more noble cause.*

The Glorious 1st Corps still fights most fearful odds, yesterday it was necessary to throw in his last resources even his engineers. But he succeeded in his task. Oh, if people had found it a little more convenient to pay deference to the warning of all Lord Roberts, if only the little army we did have had been adequately equipped for a European War – if only an army had not been a political tool. What lives would have been saved what millions and millions of money.

French soldiers

Thousands and thousands of Englishmen are today being pounded to death by guns with which we are unable to scope – why? Because they were too "expensive" to maintain in peacetime. How horrible, how revolting this bald truth seems

12TH NOVEMBER

now. The men I pity are those who were responsible and today see their hands soiled by the blood of their countrymen.

England does not yet realise that this was is a national struggle for existence. She may shake herself out of her slumbers and her childish belief in theoretical illusions about safeguarding England by her Navy!

We are all getting very tired of this continual stress and the loss of life stuns one. We are now in the trenches today for the next two days. Deluges of rain and a bitter wind. Bill Callander of the Greys was sent for by Sir John French, and was brought out of his trench mud from head to foot because he had his trench blown in on top of him.

The volunteers will be a match for the best German troops and I think that they will do better than some of our infantry even, for they are a better class of men and will be fit and able to stand the mental and physical strain. I see that the Emden (SMS Emden sunk by Australian frigate in battle of Cocos) has been sunk. I hope the commander escapes for he is a hero and has done some marvellous deeds.

T'is an odd night to see these Belgium towns absolutely desolate and deserted like Moscow in 1812.

This writing case is a great boon to me and just exactly what I wanted and enables me to scribble a line whenever there is nothing doing. Because I carry it in my saddle bag.

God Help you, you are my darling,

Yours Pedlar.

LETTERS FROM THE FRONT

14th NOVEMBER
The blackest day of Chetwode's life

Darling,

We have had a very trying day, the most appalling experience ever borne by cavalry. Chetwode (General Philip Chetwode, in charge) *says it is the blackest day of his life. Our brigade was sent to the village which became the centre of shell fire. Jardine, who was all thru the Russ-Jap war says that never has such volume of shell fire ever been seen.* (Jardine was former Military Attache to the Japanese) *1904 was child's play in comparison. Our men never fired a shot all day – but had to sustain great loss of life without the opportunity of return.*

Pedlar, General, Chetwode, Williams, Pugsy, Howes

14TH NOVEMBER

1. Holmpatrick 2. Chetwode 3. Rearsley 4. Howard Lyse. (Signed) Officer news of first cavalry division

I enclose a letter which I wrote at a moment when death was imminent, I don't want you to open it and read it until after the war. (see letter 14/9) I wrote it as I was walking back to cross as fire swept one - to take stretcher bearers to two officers who were in terrible agony. I never thought I should get back again, as there was one bridge over a canal which was being heavily shelled.

It was a horrid night to see our gallant brigade going over this filthy carnage – one man in five was hit one wounded how any escaped. Only shellfire therefore more horses than men were killed.

The village caught fire four times on account of the lyddite shell – the noise was terrific. Colonel Bulkeley-Johnson (Colonel, later General) of the (Scots) Greys is a fine man and displayed true British coolness – for his glorious regiment was mauled badly. Some gun limbers took to flight – Colonel Bulkeley seized the leading horses, pulled the driver off and hit him full between the eyes and marched him down the road and then kicked him into the gutter!

It had a very salutary effect on the others.

It has been a horrid day – we never ought to have been where we

81

were. It was a mistake in the orders owing to faulty aeroplane reconnaissance.

The day of our lives – I shall never forget it. Chetwode says it is the blackest day of his life. Because of the <u>unnecessary</u> loss of life. Our 2nd Corps was unable to make headway against a very strong rearguard position on the whole we have been successful.

We are now a component part of the 2nd Cavalry Division which is a great blow to us, as hitherto we have been independent and a very happy party.

Chetwode

Darling I always think of you my beloved one especially in moments of danger.

God bless you my angel,

Yours Pedlar.

20th NOVEMBER
32 yards from the Germans!

My Darling Beloved,

In the trenches again, and at 32 yards distant from German Trenches!! It is hardly conceivable but there it is – we had a few men (2 or 3) killed going in to the trenches and some wounded. But once in the trenches, there is little or no danger, one can hear everyone talking quite plainly.

Buddy Havoy. R.S.Q. Wounded but on duty

It is bitter winter weather now, snow all over the fields, hard frost at night and absolute hell for the wretches who have to move at night. But its better than rain – but my word it is cold.

General Bingham gave me some pills Savvys Moore anti chilblain pills which he swears cured him of the complaint. Please see about it for me and send me some in little flat cases for pocket. Also another pair of those slip soles for insertion in boot. They keep my feet warmer than anything, as the air is retained in the cells.

Last night being the coldest on earth I spent every hour taking rations and supplies up to the trenches – which job I finished at 5am! And slept until 11.30am!! during which time I gradually thawed inside the delightful flea bag.

There are some gloves I want great strong leather hedge cutting sort of gloves, also some leather ones with woollen gauntlets attached.

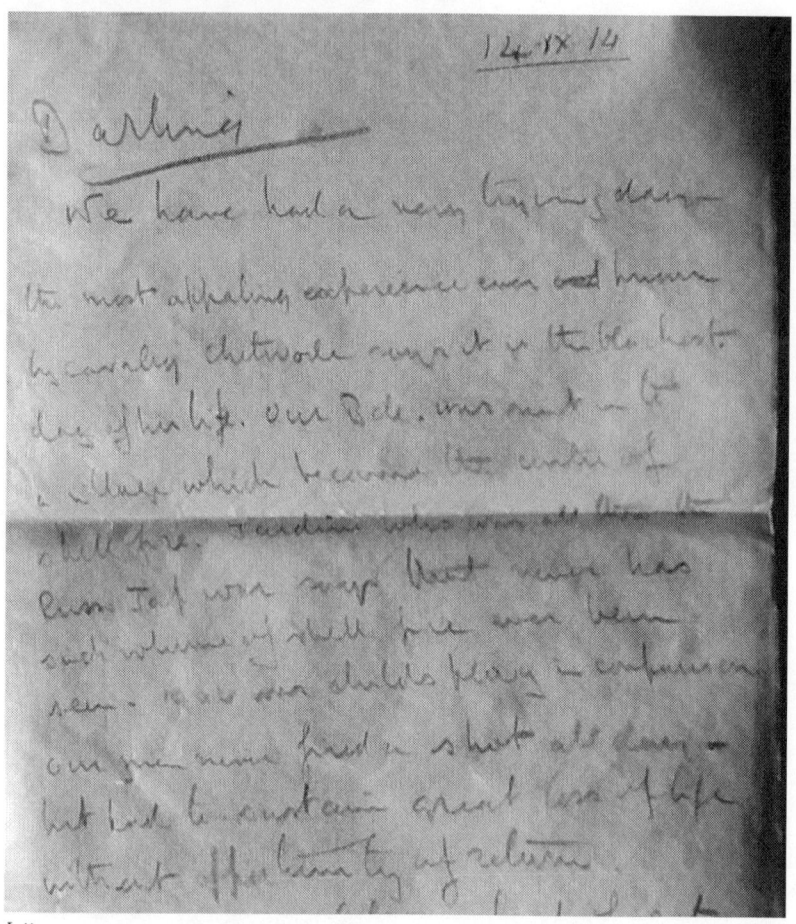

Letter

20TH NOVEMBER

There are some gloves I want great strong leather hedge cutting sort of gloves, also some leather ones with woollen gauntlets attached.

Oh Darling, How I long to see you again. I often lay awake at night thinking of my darling – perhaps I may be able to fly over to you one day soon oh what a joy if it ever comes off.

Saw Bury – looking well – he very kindly came all the way over to see me. He is interpreter to 7th Division, or some such job. He wears a worried look and I only hope they don't send him into the battalion.

I think the Germans will clear out of this very soon. It is a tedious business and I hope it will soon end. God bless you yours

Pedlar.

22nd NOVEMBER
The terrible cold

My Darling Beloved, This cold is terrible although one feels very well – but a beastly cold wind blows most of the day. There may be a chance of my popping home for 96 hours, this gives one about 2 or perhaps nearly 3 days in England. Is there room for me in your cottage. Where can I go? Or shall we go to London? It is only a dream, but in case it materialised it is as well to have some plan of campaign and not waste valuable hours trekking about.

I dare say the simplest would be to take a suite of rooms at the Ritz, where we could spend the day with the children and mother and dad could come and see one. I look at it very diffidently because of the awful parting again.

A stop to the battle the cold helped to bring

22ND NOVEMBER

Please tell Sandra to hurry up with my khaki coat, which I think you ordered some time ago one with a flannel back and circle in chest.

Just a scribble. God bless you my angel,

Pedlar.

PS Please send me ½ Ham (tinned)

24th NOVEMBER
They are all dead

My Darling Angel,

Oh the Joy to think that once again God has spared me and I really am to see my beloved one again

Before I married I had many friends, real friends. They all remained so even after I married, (a very rare occasion I can assure you). Today I have not one left alive – not one.

I have had many opportunities of seeing the 10th (Hussars) but cannot face the awful gaps which I should find. I have not the moral courage. Darling the joy of seeing you again nearly sends me crazy. I didn't sleep at all last night after I heard the good news.

You will of course arrange everything. Get me some old clothes so as I can take off my khaki and meet me in London, not at Dover unless you are sure of the hour of my return. IE if you get precise information in my letters. I may leave Calais at 9am, London 1-5pm, or Boulogne at 10.30am ...4.30pm Time arrival unknown. Will try to let you know exactly later on but shall probably leave on 26th arrive 1pm 27th London.

Oh my darling, just to lie in your arms and tell you all the awful times we have been through oh if only it was the end. Never mind, just a glimpse at you and a few hours talk is better than nothing.

Bless you,

Yours Pedlar.

26th NOVEMBER
...get at these inhuman bestial devils and wipe them out...

(post card)

My birthday!

Things move slowly here and although time is in our favour it is galling to be unable to get at these inhuman bestial devils and wipe them out and their deeds. I am gloriously well, and the rest has put me on my legs again. For the first three weeks very nearly did me in (lack of sleep and food) but we were all the same and all very highly tried, me and the staff.

Pedlar.

Reserve line French at Messines

LETTERS FROM THE FRONT

7ᵗʰ DECEMBER
50% mental casualties among officers

From Sternwerk, Flanders

Darling Beloved,

Had interesting day today, went with my general to see various people, went to Cavalry Division where we had a long talk with Allenby, then to Bulkeley Johnson's new brigade, where Sandy Hoare Ruthven is Brigade Major, then to Bungo – then to 1st Corps, then to Joey Davies' 8th Division – se we had a bit of talking.

Scots Greys at Chateau Lumigny - the turning point of Retreat

DH (Douglas Haig) was very interesting. He is terribly short of officers especially company officers. He says no one realises what his men have done- not even GHQ. The number of officers whose nerves are shattered irretrievably are very great – early 50%.

I told you a bit about the London Scottish, the Colonel (Colonel Malcolm) and another officer have now been removed! Men are still terribly shaky and are going sick at a rate of about 60 to 80 a day. However the remainder however few will be better than original regi-

ment. Raw troops cannot stand a severe reverse and the marvel is that the gallant few who did not quit were able to redeem the humour of the regiment and immortalise it.

Kavanagh was too wonderful for words. He personally rallied and led to the assault three battalions of Frenchman on three different occasions. The charge on foot of his brigade was the finest thing that has yet been done in this war, and moreover it saved the first corps.

Three times DH had to throw in his personal body guard, absolutely last available rifle, including cooks, waiters , servants, in order to endeavour to stem the rush.

I enclose a letter from Dad which is the letter of a _man_. Things are very quiet here now, and we are all bored stiff, but the rest and refitting is greatly needed.

The infantry grumble like anything if they are a week in the trenches.

We had 15 days without relief – without support – without artillery support. I say again nothing but the finest esprit de corps would have saved us from disaster. Had anyone given way we should all have had to beat an undignified retreat.

When we eventually advance it will be "undertaking the siege of Belgium" such is the words of DH. They are true and gives one an idea of the slow slow progress which is likely to take place.

The men are all beautifully clothed now consignments of British warms, fur waistcoats and beautiful warm vest and drawers have arrived. The infantry have organised great Ablution Houses. There the men go straight from the trenches. Strip and have glorious hot baths, and their clothes are plunged into boiling disinfectants. Their boots fumigated and when they have dried and been medically examined for lice etc they put on brand new clothes during all this time, their khaki is being fumigated, ironed and mended, buttons sown on etc.

Really wonderful.

I saw some of their clothes – alive with lice – a louse is a thing which in colour is like a shrimp in water. Transparent yellow. And about the size of a small ant. Some of them have to be shaved all over and dressed with oils.

Many men have got (trench foot) in the feet from standing in the wet trenches. These poor wretches are ruined men for ever. It will come out again in later life.

Boulogne is full of people like Lady Angela Forbes etc. Commonly described as "Hors"! De Combat. If you understand the witticism.

Oh how I loved my three days with you – the Happiest I have ever spent in my life.

I have the strangest conviction that I shall pull through this alive.

Yours Pedlar.

THE LETTERS FOR 1914 END HERE

Pedlar continues to write throughout the war when at the front.

On 30th June 1916, on the eve of the Battle of the Somme he writes:
> *"This is the day for me - curiously it will be a big day in history too..."*

Pedlar was evacuated out with serious stomach wounds a few days later.

LETTERS FROM THE FRONT

Pedlar by Philip de László. Note - no hands drawn as Pedlar was called from his sitting to war before De László had finished the painting.

Head Quarters Steenwerch 1915. A few miles from the front line.

This Officer Captain Palmer 10th R. Hussars has throughout the campaign and especially during the retreat from MONS performed the duties of Staff Captin which have been very arduous with the greatest zeal and devotion to duty.
    At OOSTAVERNE on OCTOBER 30th and again at the battle at WYSCHATE on 1st NOVEMBER when the brigade was attacked and forced to retire Captain PALMER displayed the greatest coolness and gallantry in conducting the Regiments to their allotted posts and in convying on the field of battle my instructions.

    RECOMMENDED for HONOUR .

Honour note.

Pedlar by Snaffles.

Major Crichton. India before World War 1.

Rare photo of Douglas Haig playing polo with Pedlar. India before World War 1.

Pedlar's funeral in 1953 at Great Somerford beside the memorial to his two sons killed fighting in WW2.

APPENDIX 1
Index to letters from the front

27	Aug	1914	letter cut by censors
5	Sept	1914	I never realised war was like this
14	Sept	1914	I may be killed at any moment
14	Sept	1914	Chetwode's concentration
15	Sept	1914	Men shot in tens
16	Sept	1914	Goodbye to the horses
23	Oct	1914	Eustace Crawley is dead
5	Nov	1914	Five days and nights without sleep
5	Nov	1914	The blackest day
6	Nov	1914	14 days holding the line
7	Nov	1914	bitter letter about comforts at home
8	Nov	1914	from Dranoutre, Belgium
12	Nov	1914	The fall of wyschate
12	Nov	1914	men of prussia sacrifice everying to take ypres
20	Nov	1914	32 yards from the German front, but quite safe
22	Nov	1914	the terrible cold
24	Nov	1914	all my friends are dead
26	Nov	1914	Birthday celebrations at the front
7	Dec	1914	Back from Leave
12	Feb	1915	Night and day on straw
12	Feb	1915	going into the trenches
16	Feb	1915	trenches full of water up to tummy - like the peninsular war
26	June	1915	Baby Julian talking!
3	Aug	1915	I shall live and I know it.
1	Oct	1915	Prince of Wales' chauffeur killed
17	Oct	1915	Trade Unions unrest
23	Nov	1915	19 for lunch in the trenches
17	June	1916	The end is in sight
22	June	1916	Love letter
30	June	1916	Today is the day (Somme)
9	July	1916	the Germans are finished
			These partings bring home to one the realities more forcibly than ever.
End	July	1916	Pedlar was invalided out with stomach wounds

Index

Aisne 21
Allenby 59, 90
Bill Callander 79
Bulkeley Johnson 90
Bury 85
Camerons 76
Carabineers 58
Chetwode 5, 6, 11, 34, 38, 40, 42, 43, 45, 56, 62, 63, 80, 81, 82
Coldstream 38
Crichton 62, 97
Dad 41, 47, 91
Douglas Haig 8, 28, 39, 90, 97
Dover 88
Dranouter 6, 69
Eustace Crawley 5, 45, 46, 56, 62
General Bingham 83
Gough 22
Grenadiers 76
Jardine 80
Joey Davies 90
John French 22, 59, 64, 79
Kaiser 59, 61
Kavanagh 91
Kitchener 22, 66, 71
London 15, 36, 38, 43, 46, 86, 88, 90

London Scottish 90
Malcolm 90
Messines 5, 8, 12, 18, 20, 21, 22, 25, 26, 47, 72, 76, 89
Morris 40
Navy 60, 65, 79
Nether Avon 69
Neuve Eglise 76, 78
Oxford Light Infantry 76
Prussia 76
Roberts 78
Sandy Hoare Ruthven 90
Shropshires 76
Sternwerk 90
Tom Guerney 63
Vailly 44
Villers Cutteret 40
Wytschate 6, 72
1st Corps 22, 61, 64, 76, 78, 90
2nd Cavalry division 47
2nd Cavalry Division 42, 82
8th Division 90
9th Lancers 11, 61, 73
12th Lancers 17, 28, 55, 63, 72

Made in the USA
Charleston, SC
10 July 2014